Make and Use

Toys

Rita Storey

WAYLAND

First published in 2009
by Wayland

© Copyright 2009 Wayland

Wayland
338 Euston Road
London NW1 3BH

Wayland Australia
Level 17/207 Kent Street
Sydney NSW 2000

Commissioning Editor: Jennifer Sanderson
Packaged for Wayland by StoreyBooks
Project maker: Rita Storey
Photographer: Harry Rhodes – Tudor Photography

Acknowledgements:
The Publishers would like to thank the following models:
Husnen Ahmad, Hannah Barton, Hannah Buckley and
Toby Whitehouse.

Picture Credits:
All photography Tudor Photography except for
page 4 top: Getty Images 2006; page 4 bottom: Getty Images/Oscar
Gustav Reylander; page 5 top: Getty Images 2007.

British Library Cataloguing in Publication Data
  Storey, Rita.
  Toys. -- (Make and use)
  1. Toy making--Juvenile literature.
  I. Title II. Series
  745.5'92-dc22

ISBN: 978 0 7502 5683 4

Printed in China

Wayland is a division of Hachette Children's Books,
an Hachette UK Company.
www.hachette.co.uk

Note to parents and teachers:
The projects in this book are designed to be made by children. However, we do recommend adult supervision at all times as the Publisher cannot be held responsible for any injury caused while making the projects.

Contents

All about toys

Today, there are many different kinds of toy to choose from. Playing with some toys means that you run and jump around, while others are more suitable for quieter play. All toys, though, are made for having fun.

ANCIENT TOYS

For thousands of years, children all over the world have been playing with toys. Before adults made toys for them, children played with everyday objects. There is evidence of stones, nuts and bones having been used as playthings in Greek and Roman times. Children in Ancient Greece and Rome also played with dolls, like the one in the picture on the right, balls, hobbyhorses and spinning tops. These toys would have been made of wood or clay.

TOY-MAKING AND TOY SHOPS

In the 1400s in Germany, carved wooden toys began to be made in large numbers. Later, other materials, such as tin and wax, were used. Toys became a lot more affordable once new ways were found to make them in factories. By the mid 1800s, a large range of toys was available in toy shops. Toys such as dolls' houses, train sets and rocking horses were often beautifully made and very expensive to buy.

Children who could not afford these ready-made toys would have played with the glass stoppers that sealed the tops of fizzy drinks bottles and rolled the iron hoops from barrels along the street.

TODAY'S TOYS

Today the range of toys available to buy has grown enormously. While crazes for new toys come and go, traditional toys such as dolls and footballs are still popular. Toys today look very different from when they were first made. Many of them, including dolls, like the one in the picture, are made of plastic.

GET STARTED!

In this book you can discover ways of making interesting toys from around the world. Try to use materials that you already have either at home or at school. For example, for the cardboard in these projects, the backs of used-up notepads, art pads and hardbacked envelopes are ideal. Reusing and recycling materials like this is good for the environment and it will save you money. The projects have all been made and decorated for this book but do not worry if yours look a little different – just have fun making and playing with your toys.

Fun yo-yo

The yo-yo was first designed in the 1920s and has remained a popular toy ever since. Yo-yo competitions are held all over the world. Adults and children perform tricks with their yo-yos to win cups and prizes.

YOU WILL NEED

jar lid, about 5cm across

stiff cardboard

pencil

pair of scissors

PVA glue

paintbrush

coloured shapes

strip of thin card, 42cm x1cm

piece thin cord 1m long

1 Put the lid on the card and draw around it. Move the lid along and draw around it again. Repeat this until you have 12 circles.

2 Cut out all the circles.

3 Glue one circle to another, until you have glued six of them together in a pile. Then do the same with the other six. Leave them to dry.

4 Stick a coloured circle onto one side of each pile of shapes. Stick on coloured shapes to decorate.

5 Roll the strip of thin card carefully around a pencil. Glue the last bit and stick it down to make a tube. Take out the pencil.

6 Put some glue on both ends of the cardboard tube.

7 Stick one end of the tube onto the centre of one of the piles of card circles.

8 Tie the cord tightly around the tube.

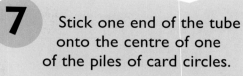

9 Stick the undecorated side of the second pile of cards on top of the tube. Wind the rest of the cord loosely around the middle of the yo-yo and tie a loop in the end for your finger.

10 Put your finger through the loop, hold the yo-yo up in the air and let it go. Just before it reaches the floor, jerk the string and the yo-yo should roll back up the string towards your hand.

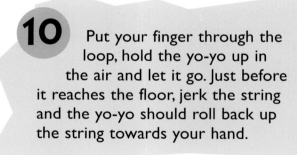

GRAVITY

When you let go of a yo-yo a force called gravity pulls it towards the floor. When you jerk the string, the energy that the yo-yo has built up on the way down, allows it to climb back up the string.

Racing bug

This simple wind-up toy uses an elastic band to make it move. As the elastic band unwinds, the bug crawls along the floor.

YOU WILL NEED

- empty cotton reel
- coloured felt
- pencil
- pair of scissors
- PVA glue
- paintbrush
- elastic band
- matchstick
- sticky tape
- stick-on eyes
- scraps of fake fur
- black felt-tipped pen

1 Draw around the end of the cotton reel onto the felt. Cut out the circle. Do the same again so that you have two circles of felt.

2 Cut a piece of felt the same width as the cotton reel and long enough to wrap around it.

3 Cover one side of the strip of felt with glue and stick it around the cotton reel.

4 Fold one circle in half and cut a small half circle from the middle. Put glue on one side of the circle with a hole in it. Stick it onto one end of the cotton reel.

5 Thread the elastic band through the hole in the middle of the cotton reel so that a loop sticks out at each end.

6 Cut a matchstick in half. Push one half through the loop in the elastic band at the end without the felt covering. Make sure that it does not stick out over the edge of the reel. Pull the elastic band from the other end so that it is pulled tight over the matchstick. Tape it in place.

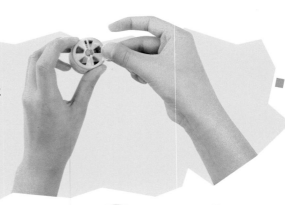

7 Using PVA glue, stick the circle of felt without the hole over the end of the cotton reel with the match in place.

8 Decorate your bug by sticking on or drawing eyes, a mouth and maybe fur or antennae.

9 Push the pencil through the loop in the elastic band. Wind up the elastic band by turning the pencil. Put the bug on a smooth surface and watch it move as the elastic band unwinds. If you make two bugs you can race them against each other.

BEASTLY BUGS

Of all the types of animal on Earth, 95 per cent are insects! Over one million different species of insect have already been discovered. Scientists think that there might be ten times that many that have not been found yet.

Jumping Jack

Jumping figures are believed to be among the earliest forms of mechanical toys. Similar toys were first made of wood thousands of years ago in Ancient Egypt.

YOU WILL NEED

piece stiff card, 21cm x 29.5cm

pencil

pair of scissors

glue

green sticky-backed paper

red sticky-backed paper

yellow sticky-backed paper

black sticky-backed paper

beige paint

red paint

black felt-tipped pen or black ballpoint pen

pencil

piece red wool, about 60cm long

large sewing needle

2 paper fasteners

large button

1 To make the shapes of a head and body draw one small and one large circle, joined together, on the stiff card. Draw a triangular shape on the stiff card to fit the head – this will be the hat. Cut out these pieces and stick the hat onto the head.

2 Draw two curving 'L' shapes on the stiff card, which will be the arms and legs. Add on two little round shapes for the hand and shape the shoes.

3 Draw around the legs onto green sticky-backed paper and cut it out. Draw around the bottom of the body circle onto the same green paper and cut it out. Stick the cut out pieces onto the legs and body. Cut out two strips of the same green paper to make braces.

4 Place the card onto the red sticky-backed paper, draw around the hat and cut out the shape. Cut straight across the bottom. Stick the shape onto the hat.

5 Draw around the arms onto yellow sticky-backed paper and cut these out. On the same paper, draw around the top of the body (cut straight across the neckline). Stick these shapes onto the arms and top of the body.

6 Cut out black sticky-backed paper feet and stick those on. Stick the braces onto the yellow top. Paint the face.

8 Push paper fasteners through the bigger holes on the braces, arms and legs. Open them out at the back of your figure.

7 Using a pencil, make a small hole in each arm and leg piece, just on the outer bend. Make a slightly bigger hole on the inner bend of each arm and leg piece and two holes on the body. Thread the needle and then pass it through the small holes on the arm and leg pieces. Leave the ends hanging for now.

9 Thread the loose ends of the wool through a button and tie a knot. Now pull on the button to make Jack jump up and down!

Beanbag frog

Children have played with stuffed toys for thousands of years. Toys can be stuffed with many different kinds of materials. This beanbag frog is stuffed with rice to make it floppy.

1 Fold the piece of paper in half and copy the shape of half a frog onto it. Cut out the shape and use it as a pattern.

2 Open out the pattern and lay it on one of the pieces of felt. Pin it in place so that it cannot move. Cut out the shape. Remove the pins and pattern.

3 Repeat step 2 with the second piece of felt.

4 Put the two frog-shaped pieces of felt on top of each other. Using backstitch (see panel), stitch all the way around the frog 1cm from the edge, following the outline. Stop sewing 3cm away from where you started.

BACKSTITCH

To sew backstitch, tie a knot in the end of the thread. Push the needle up from the back of the fabric and pull the thread through to the knot. Push the point of the needle back down through the fabric, just behind where the thread has come up. Pull it to make a stitch. Push the needle up from the back to just in front of the first stitch and pull it through. Push the needle back down to join up with the last stitch. A row of backstitches will all join up together.

5 Turn the frog inside out. To stuff the frog, fill it with rice. Do not over-stuff the frog or it will be too stiff.

6 Sew up the the gap by making stitches from the back to the front over and over again.

7 Decorate your frog by sticking on eyes or buttons and glueing on felt spots.

Racing car

Ever since the car was invented, model cars have been favourite toys. The steps below will show you how to make a magnetic car and a track to drive it around.

1 Paint a racetrack on the card. Leave it to dry.

2 Glue the four bottle tops onto the underside of the race track, one in each corner.

3 To make a car, take the tray out of one of the matchboxes. Cut a triangle shape from each side of the box.

4 To make the front of the car. Tape the top of the box to the base.

5 Flatten the outer sleeve of the second box and tape it to the back of the first box to make a 'spoiler'.

6 Using a sharp pencil, make holes in both sides of the car at the front and the back.

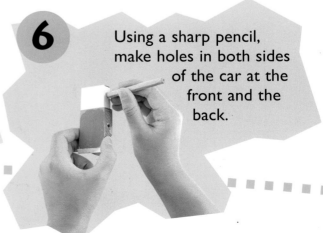

7 Paint and decorate the car.

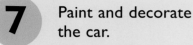

8 Cut two pieces of dowel long enough to go right through the width of the car plus 3cm.

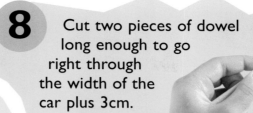

9 To make the wheels, fill the bottle tops with clay. Push the end of a piece of dowel into the centre of the clay. Then push it through the holes in the front of the box and into another bottle top, filled with clay. Do the same with the back wheels.

10 Tape one magnet to the underside of the car and the other magnet to the end of the ruler.

11 Slide the ruler under the sheet of card and move your car around the track. You could make two cars and race with a friend.

MAGIC MAGNETS

Magnets are surrounded by a force called a magnetic field. This invisible force can 'attract' the magnets (pull them toward each other) or 'repel' them (push them away from each other).
As you move the ruler the two magnets attract and pull the car round the track.

Penguin family

Stacking or nesting toys are traditionally dolls. Make a set of stacking shapes and decorate them to look like an animal or bird.

YOU WILL NEED

non-drying modelling clay
cling film
newspaper
PVA glue
paintbrush
paints

1 Cut three or four pieces of modelling clay – each one increasing in size. Roll each of the pieces into a cylinder shape. The shapes must be fatter as well as taller as they get bigger.

2 Roll the end of each cylinder under your hand to make the shape a bit narrower at the top. Stand the shapes upright.

3 Wrap each shape tightly in cling film.

RUSSIAN DOLLS

In Russia, traditional stacking dolls are called Matryoshka. There are at least five dolls in a set and sometimes many more. The dolls are made of hollow wood. Each doll opens in the middle and stacks inside each other. Traditional dolls are painted like women and children in Russian costume.

4 Tear or cut some newspaper into small pieces.

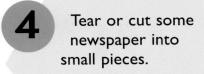

5 Mix a blob of glue with the same amount of water.

6 Stick the pieces of newspaper all over the clay figures except for the base. This is called papier mâché. Make sure that the figures are completely covered with at least three layers of papier mâché. Leave them to dry overnight. Pull on the cling film to remove the clay from the papier mâché.

7 Peel off the cling film. Paint your figures. These figures are painted to look like a family of penguins but you could choose to decorate them to look like any group of animals or birds.

Kaleidoscope

A kaleidoscope uses coloured glass and mirrors to make beautiful repeating patterns. The patterns change as you turn the kaleidoscope around.

1 Push one end out of the tube. With a sharp pencil, make a hole in the other end.

2 Cut a piece of coloured paper the same length as the tube and long enough to wrap around it. Decorate the paper with cut-out coloured shapes.

3 Put the strips of mirror face down, side by side. Using masking tape, stick the strips of mirror together.

4 Fold the pieces of mirror into a triangle. Keep the mirrored surface on the inside. Using masking tape stick the triangle together.

5 Push the mirror triangle inside the tube.

6 Cut a strip of card 2cm wide that fits round the tube and overlaps by 1cm. Glue or tape the card into a circle.

7 Cut out one circle of acetate slightly larger than the end of the tube. Stick the card circle onto the centre of the acetate circle.

8 Put the beads and sequins into the cardboard circle. Cut a circle of thin card slightly larger than the end of the tube. Stick it on top to make a box.

9 Stick the acetate base of the box with the beads inside onto the open end of the tube.

10 Look through the hole at the end of the tube and roll the tube around. You will see the shapes change as different beads are reflected in the mirrors.

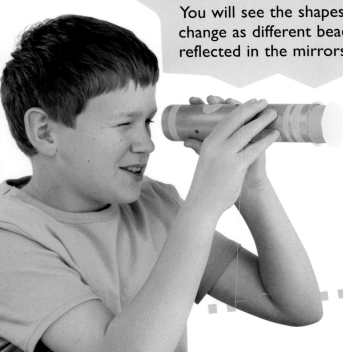

TUBE OF MIRRORS

As you look through a kaleidoscope the jumble of beads at the end are transformed into regular patterns. The mirrors inside the kaleidoscope reflect a small section of the beads, making it look as though there are six symmetrical pictures.

Carousel

The first carousel or merry-go-round was built in Europe in 1800 and was known as 'a ring of flying horses'. It became a popular attraction at fairs, seaside resorts and amusement parks.

YOU WILL NEED

a small motor

non-drying modelling clay

2 crocodile clips

3 circles of artfoam, 11cm across

2 circles of thin card, 11cm across

rolling pin

coloured paper

glue

battery in a battery holder

hole punch

5 pieces of dowel, 8cm long

1 circle of card, 12cm across

scraps of coloured paper

1 Push the motor into a ball of clay and push the clay onto a hard surface to fix it in place.

2 Connect one end of each of the crocodile clips to the connectors on the motor.

3 Make a pile with the three circles of artfoam at the top and a circle of thin card at the bottom.

4 Roll out a ball of clay 5mm thick and put it on top of the artfoam.

5 Cut a strip of coloured paper long enough to wrap around the circles. Glue it on.

6 Push the spindle of the motor through the centre of the thin card circle and into the artfoam.

7 Turn the motor over and fix the clay to a hard surface. Connect up the loose crocodile clips to the ends of the battery. The base of the carousel will start to spin.

If it is spinning too fast, add another layer of clay until it is spinning slowly. When you have the correct speed, take off one of the battery connectors.

8 Punch five holes in the remaining small circle of card. Put it on top of the clay. Push the dowels through the holes into the clay base.

9 Cut a piece of coloured paper to fit around the outside of the larger circle of card. Stick this circle on top of the dowels. Cut out horse or car shapes and stick them onto the dowels.

10 Carefully put the carousel onto the spindle on top of the motor. Connect up the loose crocodile clip to the battery and your carousel should turn. Do not run the carousel continuously.

Glossary

affordable
Something that you have enough money to pay for.

attract
When objects are pulled towards each other. The opposite poles of a magnet attach one another.

environment
Everything that surrounds us on the Earth.

felt
A type of material that is made by pressing wool together and heating it with steam.

force
A type of power that can make things move.

hobbyhorses
A stick with a horse's head, used as a toy and ridden by children.

magnetic field
An invisible force that can attract or repel other objects or magnets.

mechanical
Something that moves using machinery.

pattern
Anything made or designed to be copied many times.

recycle
To recycle something is to change it or treat it so that it can be used again.

reflected
Bounced back. Light is bounced back when it hits a shiny surface. That is why you can see yourself in a mirror.

repel
When objects push away from each other.

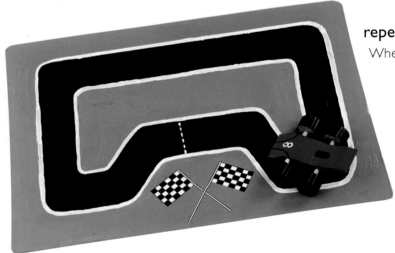

reusing

Using something for a different purpose. For example if you use cardbaord from a cereal packet to make a project, you are reusing cardboard.

species

A group of plants or animals that have things in common.

spinning tops

A toy that can be balanced on a point while it spins around.

spoiler

A device used on racing cars to break up the air around them as they move. This helps to keep the car under control.

symmetrical

An exact reflection of a structure or pattern on either side of a dividing line.

FURTHER INFORMATION

http://pbskids.org/zoom/activities/sci/
A great site with more toys to make.

www.vam.ac.uk/moc/collections/toys/index.html
This website has information about different toys through the ages.

www.scienceyear.com/under11s/index.html?page=/under11s/levers/
The science behind levers explained very clearly on this website.

Note to parents and teachers:

The website addresses (URLs) included in this book were valid at the time of going to press. However, because of the nature of the Internet, it is possible that some addresses may have changed, or sites may have changed or closed down since publication. While the author and publishers regret any inconvenience this may cause the readers, no responsibility for any such changes can be accepted by either the author or the publisher.

Index